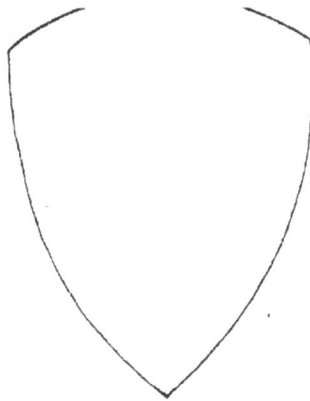

ENGLISH COPY

PARTISAN WARFARE IN CROATIA

Project #41

HISTORICAL DIVISION EUROPEAN COMMAND

OPERATIONAL HISTORY BRANCH

Published by Books Express Publishing
Copyright © Books Express, 2011
ISBN 978-1-90752-122-5

Books Express publications are available from all good retail and online booksellers. For
publishing proposals and direct ordering please contact us at: info@books-express.com

MS # P-055b

Karl GAISSER   August 1950
Colonel in the Wuerttemberg
Police Force

Project # 41b

"PARTISAN WARFARE IN CROATIA"

Translator: L. SCHAEFER
Editor   : H. HEITMAN
Reviewer : Capt B.K. HUFFORD

HISTORICAL DIVISION
EUROPEAN COMMAND

MS # P-055b

Index contained in the German copy.

MS # P-055b

The Author

Karl GAISSER
Major*
Born 17 Mar 1880
Ludwigsburg,
Wuerttemberg.

Karl GAISSER first joined the Army in 1900 as a second lieutenant of field artillery. In 1899 he underwent training at the Command and Staff School, Engers, and in 1907-08 studied Oriental languages at the University of Berlin in preparation for a career in the colonial services. In 1908 he was transferred to the Reich Colonial Office and sent to the Protectorate of Togoland, a German colony which was later incorporated into French Equatorial Africa, from which he was transferred to the Cameroons, also incorporated into French Equatorial Africa after World War I. In November 1914 GAISSER was taken prisoner by the British and sent to England, where he remained until sent to Switzerland in November 1917. He remained interned in Switzerland until July 1918, when he was released and returned to Germany.

From 1920-33 GAISSER served in the Wuerttemberg Police Force. In 1933 he resigned his position and emigrated to Brazil. There he acted as honorary-consul from 1936 to 1942 and was then repatriated to Germany together with other German diplomats. In the same year he was placed in charge of the Police Training Center, Oranienburg, Berlin, where he trained police officers and NCO's for foreign service.

From June 1943 to December 1943 GAISSER was in command of the Regular Police in Croatia, Yugoslavia, with headquarters at Zagreb, and at the same time served as advisor to the Croatian Military Police School at Bjelovar. Early in 1945 he was sent to the ZI on sick leave. He was discharged from the service in March of the same year.

---
* Last rank was Colonel of the Police Force.

CONTENTS

CLOSSARY

Organization in Berlin

Reichsfuehrer SS Himmler	Reich Commander of the SS.
Sicherheitshauptamt	National Department of Security - Office of the Reich Commander, SS Political Police.
SD or Sicherheitsdienst der SS	Security Service of the SS - executive organ of the National Department of Security and the Agencies controlled by it.
Hauptamt Ordnungspolizei	National Department of the Regular Police - The central office for all affairs of the uniformed police. It was under the jurisdiction of the Ministry of the Interior and the Reich Commander of the SS.
Schutzpolizei	Protective Police - Included the Municipal, the Rural, the Waterways and the Fire Protection Police.

Organization in Croatia

Befehlshaber des RFSS in Kroatien	The Representative in Croatia of the Reich Commander of the SS- Major General of the SS (SS Gruppenfuehrer) Kammerhofer.
Befehlshaber des Sicherheitsdienstes	Commander of the Security Service in Croatia.
Befehlshaber der Ordnungspolizei	Commander of the German Regular Police in Croatia - later re-designated the German-Croatian police. This post initially was held by a colonel of police but who was later up-graded to a brigadier general of police.

Croatian Organization

Poglavnik   Leader, the honorary title of Ante Pavelic,
                   the head of the Croatian State.

Ustasha   A nationalistic Croatian party of exiles,
                   which had its headquarters in Italy during
                   the Yugoslavian regime. Its organization
                   resembled that of the National Socialist
                   Party in Germany.

Geographical Terms

gora or gorje	-	mountain range
planje	-	mountain plateau
grad	-	city
mali	-	small
veliki	-	large
dolje	-	lower
novi	-	new

GLOSSARY

REGIONAL ORGANIZATION

There were four districts: Zagreb, Banja Luka, Osijek and
                             Sarajevo.

Each district was controlled by a District Commander(of Zagreb,
etc.), who was an SS officer with military rank equivalent to
that of colonel or brigadier general. There were also within
each district a commander of the Security Service and a commander of the German-Croatian police.

Special detachments of the Security Service, which were executive agencies of the Security Service consisting of several
interrogation groups with corresponding auxiliary units, were
stationed in all larger cities.

SS and Police Regiments - partly or fully motorized combat
units of the Protective Police were activated by the National
Department of the Regular Police (German) for combat missions,
usually behind the front. They were assigned to occupied
territories according to need.

SS Divisions, which were combat units activated by the National
Department of Security (German) for combat service at the
front. The Reich Commander of the SS had a deciding voice as
to their employment.

RULES OF PRONUNCIATION

c	-	tz,	Topolovac - Topolovatz
c	-	tsch,	Bihac - Bihatch, Pavelic - Pavelitch
s	-	sh,	Sestine - Sheshtine, Nasice - Nashitze
z	-	sh,	Kriz - Krish (at end of word)
gj	-	dj,	Gjurgjevac - Djurdjevatz.

<u>Foreword by General Franz HALDER, former Chief of</u>

<u>German Army General Staff</u>

This is a particularly valuable manuscript. Besides
presenting very informative examples of partisan warfare,
which are illustrated with excellent sketches, it provides
a good insight into the terrorist methods by means of which
a disciplined partisan organization could force into its service an inherently peaceful and anti-partisan rural popula--
tion, as well as the system and methods of command of organized
partisan bands. It also shows, however, that the partisan
threat can only be countered by systematic combat conducted
with adequate forces, and not by half-measures and improvi-
sations. Sufficiently comprehensive, systematic preventive
measures, if taken in time, can nip in the bud all attempts
to build up a partisan movement and avoid later expenditure
of effort and painful sacrifices. Effective propaganda among
the population of a region threatened by partisans plays an
essential part in such preventive measures.

/s/ Franz HALDER

Koenigstein/Taunus, 19 September 1950

Introduction by General Hans von GREIFFENBERG

The first section of the manuscript deals with the situation in Croatia as well as the military and political organization of the partisans and of the German occupation forces from 1942 on.

The second section contains tactical examples of partisan warfare presented in the form of separate narrations, in each of which the German and enemy measures and, where suitable, the practical knowledge gained thereby are set forth.

In a short concluding chapter the principal inferences that can be drawn and lessons that can be learned are again summarized. The essay is naturally not an exhaustive description of the military history of guerilla warfare in Croatia; reliable documents and maps are lacking for this purpose. It is based solely on the author's reconstruction from memory of reports and memoranda written on the basis of actual experience which he submitted at the time under discussion to the central headquarters of the Regular Police at Berlin for training purposes, and confines itself to describing the nature of the partisan war in Croatia between June

1943 and October 1944.

The partisan movement in Croatia deserves special
notice because it developed from different motives and
therefore often took on other forms than did the guerilla
warfare in Russia or in the Serbo-Graeco-Macedonian region
of the Balkans.

In Croatia, we have to do with a national structure,
newly created after the collapse of Yugoslavia, a state
which was initially more or less under Italian, but later
completely under German influence. After all is said and
done, it was an allied state, the administration and police
organs of which, though precariously established, were autonomous, and the population of which was by no means uniform
in its views. In all other theaters of war where the German
Wehrmacht came into contact with partisans, the Wehrmacht was
in enemy territory and had to assume a corresponding attitude.

The author, Police Colonel Karl GAISSER, was assigned to
the commander of the regular police in Croatia from June 1943
to November 1944 and, after an indoctrination period of three
months, was put at the disposal of the Croatian rural police
as an adviser. He personally participated in some of the
actions described.

During his term as commander of the Police School for
Service Abroad#, Oranienburg, the author had already occupied

─────────────────
Polizeischule fuer Auslandsverwendung.

himself with anti-partisan warfare. At this school he had

directed two courses, in each of which twenty-five to thirty-

five police officers and 400-500 sergeants (Wachtmeister) re-

ceived training, who were subsequently assigned to police

units in the East, the Balkans and in Africa.

Besides this, the author has had abundant practical

experience in military police service abroad, having served

for four years as a district commander in the former German

protectorate of Togoland, and with the German Army in the

Cameroons during World War I, after which he spent nine

years in the interior of Brazil.

/s/   von GREIFFENBERG

THE SITUATION IN CROATIA AFTER 1942

(See Sketch 1)

After the defeat of Yugoslavia on 17 April 1941,
Croatia at first came into the Italian sphere of influence,
Italy being interested primarily in the coast of Dalmatia
and the islands off that coast. In the spring of 1943, Italy
gave up her predominant position in Croatia, transferring
this area to German supervision but retaining her sphere of
influence on the Dalmatian coast. After the defection of
Badoglio, in September 1943, the Italian units and staffs in
Croatia which had not been previously disbanded were taken
into German custody.

The Italian measures to secure the country against
guerillas were inadequate. The will, and perhaps even the
necessary forces, to combat the guerilla threat effectively
were lacking. From Croatia came the reproach that the Italians
were intentionally lukewarm in this struggle against the
guerillas in order that they might have a reason to maintain
the occupation of the "autonomous" state of Croatia, which
meanwhile had been recognized as an ally, and thus prove the
necessity of their continued presence in the Balkans.

The hastily established Croatian state admittedly had

quickly covered the land with a net of administrative offices
and police stations copied from the Italian model, but military units capable of being used in combat came into creation
only gradually. Since the administration was directed by the
Ustasha, which was highly disliked in the country and was
supported at most by one-tenth of the population, and since
the Ustasha considered its prime mission to be the suppression
of its political opponents within the Croatian towns, the
guerilla bands forming in mountain nests were not seriously
threatened but could work at their organization and systematically extend the areas under their control.

When the German police took over the protection of the
country in the spring of 1943, the partisans controlled the
Bosnian Karst to the line Slunj - Bihac - Kljuc - Gorika
Vakuf, and north of the Save river the ridges of the Bilo
gora and of the Papuk, the heart of the Fruska gora and
smaller border regions. Roads close to these areas could only be used under protection of an escort. From 1944 on,
Tito's partisans received their supplies from the Allies in
increasing measure by air drop and by sea. With the fall of
Belgrade in the autumn of 1944, the front reached Croatian
territory.

The Croatian population at first had welcomed German in-
tervention, since they expected therefrom more effective pro-

tection than the Italians had vouchsafed them against the
mounting partisan activity. The more evident it became that
the initiative was passing to the partisans, in consequence
of German weakness, the greater were the numbers that went
over to the partisans. In the summer of 1944, even university
students from Zagreb served for months in nearby partisan
territory while allegedly spending the vacation with country
relatives. The desire to seek favor with the Tito party
against the event of a German defeat gradually seized the
entire upper strata of the Croatian bourgeoisie, whose guiding
principle was to avert or at least to limit the destruction of
Croatian property.

PARTISAN ORGANIZATION IN CROATIA
(See Sketch 1)

A partisan group, the Chetniks, had formed in Serbian territory from dispersed elements of the former Yugoslavian Army. The Italian commanders did not fight it energetically, and there were even several instances of mutual toleration. At the defection of Badoglio, toleration developed into open support of the Chetniks through the sale of weapons. In Bosnia, the Chetniks were also on South Croatian soil. In the beginning they were treated forbearingly.

Independent of this group and in open opposition to it because of its encroachment on Croatian territory, a Croatian partisan group had developed under the leadership of Josip Bros, alias Tito, a Croat educated in Moscow. In a short time, this group had placed itself in sole possession of the Grmec mountain region and from there proceeded to organize the partisan movement in Bosnia and Dalmatia and on both sides of the Save river.

The objectives of the partisan movement were separated into clearly defined phases. First efforts were directed at establishing areas in the most remote forest and mountain regions in which the partisans could build up their organization without interference. The next phase was the expansion

of these areas. More and more villages were drawn into the
partisan-controlled area, so that the partisans could live
off them and also to prevent manpower and provisions from
aiding the German war effort. As a result, recruiting for
German units and the provisioning of those units and the
Croatian territory protected by them rapidly became more and
more difficult. The objectives which have been outlined above
led to combat against all German and Croatian forces committed
for partisan warfare. The tactical principle followed by
the partisans was to retreat whenever the enemy was superior
in strength, even if this meant that temporarily they had to
abandon their principal hiding places.

After the autumn of 1943, the initiative passed into
the hands of the partisans. German and Croatian protective
units were attacked in increasing measure, and the partisan
sphere of influence was extended to the vicinity of the larger
cities and the principal lines of communications, which were
protected by the Wehrmacht. The all-out attack on these vital
lines was the last phase. In its timing, it coincided with
the retirement of the front line of battle to Croatia in the
autumn of 1944. The inclusion of this line of battle in the
partisan territory concluded the war of extermination against
the foreign invader.

In accordance with the objectives already stated, the

partisan organization was active in the following three
fields:

1. The administration of the area dominated by partisans.

2. The formation, in regions not yet dominated, of an
underground net, which assumed functional duties when the
region was drawn into the partisan controlled area.

3. The activation and maintenance of combat units in
the partisan-held area, and the employment of these units
outside this area.

Ad 1. Administrative agencies, which took Croatian
characteristics into consideration but were modelled on the
Russian original, were set up in all areas in which the partisans had complete control. These bodies were run by political
commissars, and, besides satisfying the need of the partisans
themselves, their function was to care for the poorer sections of the population at the expense of the more well-to-do.
In the primary phase, they also had the function of local
headquarters. Communist-Titoist propaganda was immediately
disseminated. Walls and the sides of houses were plastered
with suitable posters.

Ad 2. The developemnt of an underground net in any
region was always preceded by the establishment of hideaways
in the highest and most inaccessible parts of wooded mountain
ranges. From such a hideout, recruiters scoured the vicinity

far and wide, sought out secret collaborators and pledged
them to help the partisans.

The first objects of attack were the smallest settle-
ments, those which were situated far up at the heads of the
highest valleys. In effect, the plan of operations was always the same. About midnight, some village outside the
partisans area would be surrounded. The village streets
would be secured by patrols and the delivery of provisions
and stores demanded. Through the windows of the houses was
passed the command, "Make no noise. Come to the door." Then,
"In an hour we shall take a ham, five loaves of bread, a
kilogram of butter, twenty eggs, a wicker-bottle of wine
and a sheet." Later the requisitions were extended to all
sorts of necessary articles, including building materials
and manpower. Carefully prepared lists were drawn up for
the collections by secret party members. The leaders on the
spot were always party members from other villages, so that
the party members of the same village would not be revealed.
Contributions were levied only from well-to-do people, and
no more was requisitioned than the group could carry away
immediately. After the booty had been collected, after three
or four hours at the most, the whole band disappeared noise-
lessly from the village. Resistance was impossible and was
not attempted. In most cases not even a report of the incident

reached the proper Croatian authorities. If the general
situation permitted, the village which had been tamed in
this manner was then incorporated into partisan territory.

Ad 3. The mobile combat unit of the partisan was the
battalion, about 300-400 strong. As a rule, such small for-
mations also were called brigades. Later, divisions and
corps also appeared, but these designations hardly aided
in determining their combat strength.

The training was very severe, and iron discipline was
enforced. Unconditional obedience was demanded, and punishment was determined by a group of comrades designated by the
leader. A shot through the back of the neck was no unusual
punishment for cowardice and traitorism. The execution was
carried out before the assembled unit by the one next in line
to the offender.

Equipment was as simple as can be imagined, consisting
of a civilian suit with or without insignia, a gun and
ammunition. The men went barefoot or wore opanken, sandal-
like Serbian footwear. They slept on the bare ground and
in the open when no huts were available. Besides their own
equipment, the men had also to carry the necessary supplies.
Organic combat trains appeared only in the later, more developed stages. Natives, including women, and prisoners of
war were used as carriers.

Great value was placed upon ability in night marching. Marches of forty kilometers per night for several nights in succession, along paths and with full loads, were the normal performance required of a battalion. In this way the transfer of a unit from the Bosnian mountains to the massif north of the Save was possible in two or three nights. The routes were carefully reconnoitered. On principle, only footpaths and hunting or sheep trails were used. The detachments marched in single file, avoiding villages. From sector to sector the commanders located the local underground, which had been reported by couriers. Main communication lines were crossed vertically and whenever possible at night, with special security measures and in out-of-the-way places, while streams were forded in the most remote spots. The day's rest then followed, deep in the woods or in some partisan village.

The Bosnian mountains offered extensive protection but little chance for collecting provisions, and so the first recognizable operational objective of the partisans was to procure food for the men concentrated there. Brigades, in battalion strength, were slipped out of this region into the region north of the Save. There they fattened themselves for three weeks on requisitioned food and then, heavily loaded with provisions, were rotated with new brigades, which brought with them ammunition as well as medical and technical supplies.

Since no effective countermeasures were taken against these
developments, exceptionally capable partisan combat units
and extensive partisan areas developed in the manner described
above. Special features of combat training were firing
discipline, exploitation of forest, bush and other terrain
cover, quick movements, carefully contrived assaults and
noiseless disengagement from the enemy. The dispersion of
entire units, filtration through enemy lines and the art of
remaining in individual concealment while the enemy forces
passed, in order then to re-assemble at some distant meeting
point, were forms of movement that were completely mastered.

GERMAN ORGANIZATION AND BATTLE COMMAND
(See Sketch 1)

The following German agencies were in Zagreb in the summer of 1943:

The German general accredited to the Croatian Government, General von Glaise-Horstenau.

The accredited representative of the Reich Commander of the SS, Major General of the SS Kammerhofer.

The German ambassador, Major General of the SA Kasche. Each received his instructions from a different office, von Glaise-Horstenau from the Wehrmacht High Command, Kammerhofer from the National Department of Security*, which was controlled by Himmler, and Kasche from the Foreign Office, controlled by von Ribbentrop. The autonomous state of Croatia had its own war department, and the Croatian rural and regular police were under the authority of the Department of the Interior. Both departments received detailed instructions from Ante Pawelic, the clever and versatile Poglavnik, or Chief of State, a Croatian nationalist who maintained an attitude of reserve toward Italy and who was pro-German and anti-Serbian. The collaboration of these four groups revolved around a division of duties, each group endeavoring to avoid responsibility for the most unpleasant tasks.

* Sicherheitshauptamt

The principle responsibility of the Wehrmacht* was the protection of the Cilly - Zagreb - Belgrade railway line, which was the major supply line to Greece. Of secondary importance were the branch lines Zagreb - Ogulin - Susak and Brod - Sarajevo - Mostar - Dubrovnik and Vinkovci - Osijek. Only territorial reserves** and training units were permanently assigned, combat troops being assigned temporarily according to requirements.

The actual mission of combatting the partisans was the responsibility of the German-Croatian police, an assignment which they shared with the Croatian State. The organization of the German-Croatian police was based upon Croatian provincial and county divisions. It was divided into a security service and a uniformed regular police force. The representative of the Reich Commander of the SS was supported by the commanders of the security service and of the regular police. Four districts were established, each with a district commanding officer, with headquarters in Zagreb, Banja Luka, Osijek and Sarajevo. Bihac was intended to be a fifth district, but it fell into the hands of the partisans before its organization was completed. The district commander in each district was

---

*   German Armed Forces.
**   Landsturm I and II, trained and untrained reserves over forty-five years of age.

a senior SS officer with the rank of SS brigadier general
(Brigadefuehrer), who actually had full command authority
within his zone and was responsible for all operations. Commanding officers of both the security service and the regular
police served under him. Initially these posts were held by
officers with the rank of major or lieutenant colonel, but
later the rank was raised to that of colonel.

The security service supervised political developments
in the country. Its principal duties were the collection of
reports and the prosecution of political opponents. Its executive agencies consisted of several interrogation groups.
Its personnel were national and ethnic* Germans. The regular
police organized combat troops, carried out security and combat instructions and provided protection for the operations
of the Security Service. It was led by German gendarme or
police officers, and each company contained six to eight German gendarme or police technical sergeants /Wachtmeister7, with
Croatian enlisted men. Croats who had received appropriate
training in the Yugoslavian service could also serve as officers
and non-commissioned officers.

The Croats were good fighters and knew the country, and
some of them had received military training. Interpreters
chosen from among the ethnic Germans maintained liaison with

* Volksdeutsche - Foreign nationals of German extraction.

the Croatian personnel. Each squad was supposed to have an interpreter, but often a platoon had only one or two. All Croats who served as officers could speak German. As a rule the German officers and non-commissioned officers came directly from the gendarme and police services in Germany. Their training for partisan combat consisted of service with the Army in World War I, a three or four month training course at a gendarme or police school and the exercise of their occupation in the ZI or in occupied territories. The company commanders and the non-commissioned officers were very often over-age.

The formation of the units progressed step by step, and replacements were continuously fed to the headquarters. The desire to adapt themselves to the Croatian administrative organization resulted in headquarters' funneling the replacements that came to them right on to the larger county centers. There companies were formed for training and to augment the combat strength of the local Croatian gendarme posts, whom they were to support in combatting the partisans in the county zone. Posts in platoon strength were placed in endangered villages by the companies.

A larger county town could be described somewhat as follows. The administration was handled by the Croatian prefect, who was supported by a bodyguard of Ustashas as well as by a Croatian gendarme station of from twenty to forty

men. These latter performed police duties in much the same
way as the Italian Carabinieri. Physically separated from
them, a German-Croatian police company, under the command of
a district first or second lieutenant, was quartered in a
schoolhouse, brewery or some such building, which was protected
by barbed wire and window barricades. It served primarily as a
training center. Around the police barracks, the daily life
in the city of 8,000-10,000 inhabitants proceeded as it had
in peacetime.

The equipment of the police companies was at first very
primitive. It consisted chiefly of captured long French
rifles, one or two light machine guns and some submachine
guns. All means of transportation, including field kitchens,
had to be improvised. The most that could be reasonably expected of such a company was the protection of its own center
and of areas within a radius of twenty kilometers. The quality
of its training depended in decisive measure on the training
and military proficiency of the post commander, who had to
feel his way carefully in working out his line of action.
Supervision and guidance by the responsible commander of the
regular police was limited to general directions and occasional
short inspection tours. After the defection of Badoglio, which
made possible the seizing of Italian stocks, the equipment
situation improved.

All outpost units of company strength or less were
welcome targets for partisan attacks, and many men were lost
in such attacks. They were the ones that bore the brunt of
Himmler's order that under no circumstances was any position
to be given up without his express permission. The permission
never arrived at the right time.

It was only after numerous reports had been sent in that
Berlin recognized the necessity to activate combat troops in
regiments and much time passed before these regiments were
ready for action. Once the front line of battle reached
Croatian soil they had to be moved into action there, but
during the training phase they played an effective part in
resisting local partisan pressure in the localities where they
were stationed.

The Croatian state had two organizations intended for
anti-partisan combat, namely, the Croatian Army and the Croatian rural police. The Croatian Army, at first with Italian
and later with German support, activated regiments of the
mountain infantry type, which fought at endangered points with
laudable aggressiveness in spite of inadequate equipment. They
were used primarily in Bosnia and Dalmatia, and from 1944 onward
combat divisions were trained on German troop training grounds
and then sent to the front. The Croatian rural police manned
smaller gendarme posts, spread out over the county. The personnel,
the majority of whom had been taken over from the Yugoslavian

area and trained by experienced gendarme officers of imperial
Austrian mintage, had a wide knowledge of the region and its
people, were trusted by them and were efficient. They gave
the German-Croatian police units valuable assistance during
operations. Beyond that, however, the posts, as executive
instruments of the Croatian government, were tied to their
own area. As far as the Croatian police in the larger cities
were concerned, there was no question of using them in combat
against the partisans.

The Ustasha, the political party of the Poglavnik, also
activated combat forces, of which small units devoted themselves,
in a manner similar to the German security service, to combatting their Yugoslavian opponents, an action which did not
increase the popularity of the ruling party. In 1944, first
one and then two divisions were activated as an elite guard,
the bodyguard of the Poglavnik. These units performed well
in anti-partisan action in the Zagreb - Varazdin - Koprivnica -
Bjelovar region.

After the summer of 1943, the battle command against the
partisans was in the hands of the representative of the Reich
Commander of the SS, who then co-ordinated the measures of the
Croatian government with his own aims, while adapting those
aims to the limits drawn by the Armeegruppe# in Belgrade.

Headquarters of the reinforced German army stationed in
   Yugoslavia.

Air forces appeared only in isolated cases in 1943. The
airport in Zagreb was under German and Croatian administration
and served as a transit field and for passenger traffic. One
solitary Fieseler Storch* was available to the SS representative
in 1943, and not until the following spring was there assigned
to Zagreb a small bombardment wing, which, among other things,
joined in the fighting around Banja Luka.

In the beginning, the security of the Adriatic was Italy's
responsibility. After Italy's defection in 1943, the patroll-
ing of the coast was organized from Trieste by the Germans,
but ammunition and supplies could not be prevented from reach-
ing the partisans.

* German liaison plane.

TACTICAL EXAMPLES FROM THE PARTISAN WAR
(See Sketch 2)

Combing the Bilo Gora and the Papuk, 6-18 July 1943

The Situation

The realization that something decisive had to be done
to hinder the establishment of guerilla bands in the wooded
mountain ranges north of the Save led to a major drive in
July 1943 against the Bilo gora and the Papuk, an attack
which was planned and executed by the Wehrmacht. A regiment
of the partially motorized 100th Light Infantry Division was
made available on short notice by the Wehrmacht High Command
for this purpose. A training battalion of the Wehrmacht
from Bjelovar and one from Brod also participated in the
operation, as well as several Croatian Army units, operational
units of the security service, German-Croatian police companies
from the districts of Zagreb and Osijek and Croatian gendarme
units.

The territory held by the partisans extended from Nosti,
fifteen kilometers south of Koprivnica, in a southeasterly
direction over the forest slopes of the Bilo gora to the Papuk
mountain range, which was regarded as its center. Several
partisan brigades which were fit for combat had been reported
in the Papuk. The Moslavacka gora and the Psunj were outlying

partisan bases. The railway lines Zagreb - Brod - Belgrade
and Vinkovoi - Osijek were in operation. Partisan underground activity was to be expected in greater or lesser degree in the whole region adjoining the partisan controlled
areas.

The Objective

To clear the Bilo gora and the Papuk of guerilla bands.

Command

The commander of the 100th Light Infantry Division,
Brigadier General von Axt, with headquarters first at Kopri-
vnica and later at Virovitica, which was protected by a
Croatian Army battalion.

The Plan of Operations

Once the foreground had been cleared, the 54th Rifle
Regiment, which had been reinforced to four-battalion strength,
was to begin with the Glogoveo - Kriz - Topolavac - Kapela -
Hampovica - Gjurgjevac sector and then systematically to comb
the Bilo gora section by section with the aid of one battery
and one company of engineers. Croatian and German units were
to clear out the foreground to the west and southwest and force
the partisans into the pocket formed by the rifle regiment.
The partisans were to be driven from all sides toward the
center of the Papuk range in synchronized movements. The
Koprivnica - Virovitica - Djakovo - Osijek highway, north of

the Bilo gora, and the Zagreb - Ivaniograd - Novska - Brod
rail line, south of the range of wooded mountains, were to
serve as supply routes.

Results Achieved

Since the net was too widely meshed and the number of
troops too small, the partisans, after some initial resistance, escaped encirclement in all directions through the
dense forest. Not a single partisan was caught in the net,
and only surprised civilians were taken prisoner. Since the
combing operation was carried out in a single wave, it was
extremely easy for the partisans to re-assemble behind it.

HOW THE 54TH RIFLE REGIMENT PERFORMED ITS MISSION

The regiment had been assigned a training battalion and thus reinforced to four battalions. It was divided into two groups, one of which was to form a cordon while the other carried out the combing. The group designated for the combing operation carried light combat equipment and advanced on a broad front at right angled to the contour of the mountain chain, moving over the intervening hills to the blocking line where its motorized train awaited it. After the arrival of the combing unit, the motorized blocking unit swiftly moved ahead down the valley to the new blocking line around the next sector. Excessive fatigue on the part of either group was avoided by alternating these assignments. The narrower sides of the sector were closed off by special detachments, which participated as needed in the job of driving the partisans into the pocket. For the combing operations, specific routes and objectives were assigned to the individual companies, which advanced in a direct line on the ordered objectives with their flanks secured. No thorough search of the combed region could be made, as the day's objective had to be reached and the number of participating troops was not sufficient for such action. There were gaps all over in the line, through which the par-

tisans could slip out or in which they could hide until the
drive had passed.

THE TACTICS OF THE PARTISANS

At various villages on the perimeter of their area which had already been organized as bases and contained supply depots, the partisans at first offered energetic resistance, tactically well prepared but primitive in respect to materiel. The superior weapons of the Wehrmacht, especially the light and medium mortars and heavy machine guns, soon forced the partisans to give up combat. It seems that they originally aimed at concentrating all their combat units in the Papuk mountains, but when they saw that they were not equal to the German troops in combat they limited themselves to blocking paths in the mountains in order to delay the advance of vehicles. Supply depots were camouflaged excellently, e.g., a completely equipped surgical room was discovered in a vault hidden under a dungheap. The German troops were eluded, and when the center of the Papuk range had been encircled the partisan units had already filtrated the encircling line and had re-assembled in distant hideaways. The troops went to great trouble to remove the road barriers and make the roads passable. Zvecevo, the last mountain settlement, was found abandoned when the German troops had worked their way up to it on the 15th of July. There was no trace of the enemy.

On the 18th, the trains were ready for the rail trans-

portation of the regiment to the Saloniki sector in Greece.
The partisans knew the deadline for the assembly of these
transports several days before the conclusion of the operation and when moving out of their quarters in the Papuk in-
formed the population that they would probably be back soon.
Their return was prompt, and all members of the civilian
population who had supported the German troops, even if such
support had been limited to billeting, had to expect reprisals
and therefore became unquestioning followers of the partisans
in order to escape worse consequences.

With the withdrawal of the Wehrmacht, the thirteen-day
operation collapsed. The German and Croatian troops who had
been committed returned to their stations, and the combed
territory was open for reoccupation by the partisans. It
remained impenetrable for German and Croatian troops, and
the population swore complete allegiance to Tito. A great
expenditure of work, materiel, time and manpower had been
wasted.

At the conclusion of the Papuk operation, the Poglavnik
announced an amnesty for all Croats who had belonged to the
partisan movement, but this maneuver met with very little
success.

The Flaw in the Planning

Defensive action to prevent the reoccupation of the

combed areas by the partisans, an operation which was really much more important, should have been prepared and executed with the same care with which the combing operation was planned and carried out. A separate police group of several battalions should have followed the combat troops into the partisan territory as it was combed. There they should have permanently occupied the positions which the partisans had held previously and hunted down the dispersed partisans. What the Papuk range had been for the partisans, it should have become for their pursuers in anti-partisan combat. The primitive artillery range and drill field which the partisans had on the level plain atop the Papuk, an area which actually was very well suited for such purposes, should have become a training ground for German and Croatian troops.

THE CAPTURE OF THE SIGNAL COMMUNICATION PLATOON OF THE 54TH RIFLE REGIMENT AT PIVNICA ON 13 JULY 1943

(See Sketch 3)

Coming from Vorovitica during the Bilo gora combing operation, the headquarters staff and one battalion of the 54th Rifle Regiment had spent the night of 12/13 July in Pivnica. Early on the 13th, this combat force advanced to Darivar. The departure was set for 0400, and the 227th Wehrmacht Training Battalion, which had spent the night in Jasenas, was to occupy Pivnica by 0430 hours. The regiment waited for the arrival of the 227th Training Battalion in Pivnica and departed at about 0440 hours. During the march, the regiment's signal communication platoon, which contained about forty German soldiers, removed the telephone line which had been laid to Darivar the day before. Rearguard security was the responsibility of a company of the battalion, which company had spent the night in Mali Pivnica. Just as this company, then about a kilometer from the signal communication platoon, turned into the main road to Darivar, it was met by fire coming from a strip of woods west of the road and forced to take cover. At the sound of fighting, the 227th Training Battalion deployed infantry from Pivnica against the strip

of woods, but they also were fired upon and were only able
to work their way forward slowly. Similar fire was directed
against the retiring regiment from a wooded stretch to the
southwest.

The signal communication platoon, which was at work removing the telephone line in the intervening section, was over-
run by the partisans. Some of them were killed and some, who
surrendered, were separated into groups to carry the signal
materiel. The horses were unharnessed and the wagons plundered
and set afire.

Fifteen or twenty minutes later the rifle fire slackened
and died away, and when the German forces reached the scene
of the surprise attack it was empty except for the burning
wagons and a few dead German soldiers who had been stripped
of their uniforms and equipment. The partisan unit had disappeared with the booty and the prisoners in the direction of
Crnivrh. A small pursuit detachment found more dead German
soldiers in the forest and discontinued the chase.

What happened? The following explanation is probable:
One of the partisan units, which was withdrawing from the
fighting in the Bilo gora, tried to break through the German
lines and reach the Papuk massif. Unknown to the German, it
had spent the night of the 12th/13th in and about Ivanovo Selo
and from there had stolen down to the road between Pivnica and

Daruvar in order to cross it in the direction of Vocum at
the proper moment and so get into the Papuk mountains. To
cover their men while crossing the road, the partisans first
occupied the edges of the forest along the road and observed
the traffic upon it. When they realized that the signal platoon was busy removing the wires without immediate protection,
they determined to attack from the nearby woods and proceeded
to carry out the attack in a masterly manner.

The success of the surprise attack can be attributed to
the quick decision and the daring of the partisan leader and
the excellent teamwork of his followers. The attack was favored
by the terrain and the forest cover. The counteraction by the
numerically far superior German troops came too late. It
took too long for the marching battalion to halt, to recognize
the danger its signal platoon was in and to deploy for counteraction. The training battalion, which at first did not take the
shooting seriously, lost a time likewise. The rearguard company had evidently loitered. No German unit could see the
spot where the attack took place. It lasted twenty minutes
at the most, and the partisans moved with catlike speed. The
village of Ivanovo Sel was burned to the ground.

THE MOPPING UP OF THE FRUSKA GORA BY THE 9TH SS AND
POLICE REGIMENT BETWEEN 24 JULY AND 3 AUGUST 1943
(See Sketch 2)

In July 1943, the 9th SS and Police Regiment, which was partially motorized and had three battalions and supporting arms, was quartered in Ruma and the surrounding villages with the objective of combatting the partisans in the lowlands of the Save and the Fruska gora. The operation was directed by the district commander of Osijek, whose security service unit had collected data and ascertained the names of supporters of the partisan movement.

Various villages in the lowlands of the Save were known to be infected by partisans and used as a protective screen for the crossing of the river. They and nearby forest areas were surrounded and searched. Counteraction by the partisans was slight and consisted for the most part of barriers placed on the route of approach, which, due to the marshy terrain, could not be easily bypassed. Most of these barriers were not defended but nevertheless caused a certain amount of delay. There were only isolated cases of partisan fire from the woods.

All attempts to take the partisans by surprise failed, and the population found time to flee into the swamps or across the Save with their primitive possessions, only very

old people, invalids and children remaining behind in the
villages. Small supply dumps fell into the hands of the
troops.

After 31 July, the operation was diverted toward the
Fruska gora, on the ridge of which partisan combat units were
said to be staying in forest camps and isolated farmhouses.
The regiment entered the first villages of the Fruska gora
on the Ruma side without meeting any resistance, but the
operation aiming at pocketing the partisans on the ridge, .
which was staged on 1 August, proved a failure. The 1st
Battalion, which had been committed from the Ruma side, did
reach the inner encirclement ring on time, after putting
several snipers out of action and suffering losses in the
process, but the two motorized battalions committed to carry
out the envelopment lost time because of road barriers and
could make only incomplete contact with the 1st Battalion.
As had been the case in the Papuk, they found an empty nest.
The partisans had slipped through the encirclement lines in
small bands and had scattered about the Danube and Save
lowlands.

Before any further pursuit of the partisans could be
undertaken, the regiment received orders to retire to Ogulin
in order to take over from the defecting Italians the protection of the Zagreb - Ogulin - Susak railroad in that region.

There it was trapped and only after several weeks freed by
an SS division from the region around Karst, southeast of
Trieste.

After the regiment had retired from the Fruska gora,
the majority of the population fled from the surrounding
villages and took refuge in Ruma. The partisan bands, which
had reassembled quickly, returned to the Fruska gora and
took revenge on the property of the ethnic Germans, who had
fled.

The police action against the Fruska gora suffered from
the same mistakes as the Wehrmacht action against the Bilo
gora and the Papuk. Both were able to report, "Mission
accomplished. Region cleared of guerillas. All resistance
crushed. Our losses small, enemy losses heavy." Later reports, however, established that the combed area returned
to partisan hands after the troops had withdrawn and the
enemy losses were chiefly imprisoned civilians. As a logical
consequence of these supplementary reports, no further similar
operations were staged to combat the partisans in Croatia.

By September 1943, the partisans felt so strong that they
took the offensive on all sides and forced the German troops
to go on the defensive. Then followed the period of attacks
on outlying detachments and acts of sabotage against corps
and lines of communication.

ATTACK ON THE GARRISON OF CASINCI
(See Sketch 4 & 2)

Time

Late harvest, early September 1943. Weather warm; slight showers at rare intervals.

Situation

Combat units of the partisans were in the Papuk and in the country adjacent to it in the southeast. The Croatian government was in control in Djakovo, Nasice and Pozega. Traffic had been possible hitherto only within a circumscribed area and under armed escort. Occasionally the partisans controlled the traffic on the highways, and they interfered repeatedly with the harvesting, carrying off into partisan territory crops that were ready for transportation and burning threshing machines. One German-Croatian police battalion of three companies was present in Djakovo, to which it had been advanced from Osijek with the general mission of protecting the harvest. Each company had two light machine guns and a number of sub-machine guns. The men not so armed carried rifles. The partisans had similar arms but not in equal numbers. From Djakovo the police battalion detached one company to Satnica, and this company sent a platoon to Casinci at the request of a member of the Croatian Parliament to protect his estate there.

The platoon, consisting of about fifty men, moved
into Casinci and barricaded its quarters in the administrative
enclosure of the estate. It protected the field workers in
the countryside during the day and guarded the estate at
night. On Saturday evening the quarters were fired at, and
the platoon spent the night ready for action within its defensive positions. Sporadic surprise fire was received during the night. A runner, who had managed to slip out at
night through an adjacent building, carried a report of the
situation to the company in Satnica, which started for
Casinci at daybreak but came under fire at the Bosut river,
where it found the bridge blown. At about 0800, by which time
the company had fought its way clear, stragglers from the
platoon in Casinci met it and reported that their quarters
had caught fire early in the morning and that at the same
time the partisans had attacked from all sides. It had been
impossible for the platoon to remain in the burning building,
and the individual members attempted to make a break for it.
At least 400 partisans were in the village.

The company thereupon returned to Satnica, in order to
fend off a possible attack on that village, and then communi-
cated with the battalion in Djakovo. The battalion had alerted its two other companies but did not dare to advance into
the countryside, because partisans had been reported in the

vicinity of the road to Major and the battalion feared
an attack upon Djakovo from this direction. To the Catholic
battalion commander the immediate protection of the administrative center and episcopal seat seemed the most important
mission.

During the morning, a reconnaissance patrol sent out by
the company in Satnica in the direction of Casinci, in order
to bring in further survivors of the platoon which had been
stationed there, confirmed the fact that Casinci was still
occupied by strong partisan units. Inhabitants who had fled
from the village reported in Djakovo on Sunday afternoon
that the partisans, having taken along all transportable
supplies and having destroyed the house of the member of
parliament, had withdrawn to the mountains. The member of
parliament was with his family in Zagreb at the time. Only
twenty men of the platoon, including eight wounded, managed
to escape, some of them with the aid of the village inhabitants.

The battalion commander, who was unable to march because
of an attack of sciatica, was sentenced in December to four
years' imprisonment by a Zagreb SS and Police court for fail-
ing to take effective action with the two companies that were
in Djakovo to help the platoon in Casinci. The Reich Commander of the SS reversed the judgment and demanded the death
sentence. Since the battalion commander had already been

transported to a penal unit in Danzig, further proceedings
continued there, and the final result was never known.

    A captured partisan order read as follows:

Commander X   Fauoje, Friday, 0500 hours.

Order

1. On Sunday morning the village of Casinoi will be taken,
the police platoon stationed there will be destroyed and the
harvest will be carried off.

2. The 1st Battalion of the 43rd Brigade will leave Fauoje
at 1500 on Saturday and advance along forest trials to Casinoi
so as to surround the quarters of the police platoon in the
estate at the edge of Casinoi at dusk and seal off the village
of Casinoi from the outside. Inhabitants will not be permitted to leave their houses and may show no light. Window shutters
must be closed. Patrols will maintain surveillance within the
village.

During the night harrassing fire will be directed at the police
quarters, The attack will commence at dawn. The police quarters will be burned to the ground.

3. Two companies of the 2d Battalion, 43d Brigade, will leave
Fauoje at 1400 on Saturday, advance along forest trails and
arrive at the heights between Casinoi and the Djakovo - Majar
road by 1700 at the latest. They will there take up concealed
positions against Casinoi and the Djakovo - Majar road. Break-
outs from Casinoi will be prevented. Fire will be opened on the
Djakovo - Majar road only if German troops are moving on it.

4. The staff and two companies of the 2d Battalion, 43d Brigade, will cover the village of Levanjska Varos from Saturday
evening at 1800 on.

5. The 3d Battalion, 43d Brigade, will leave Slatinik at 1400
on Saturday. Two companies will be so deployed on the hills
between the Bosut river and Bracevoi that they will be able to
block the road from Satnica - Bracevoi in both directions as
soon as German troop movements occur upon it. The battalion
staff and two companies will reach the heights west of the
Bosut at the fall of dusk. German troop movements from Djakovo
will be met with fire. Any advance toward Casinoi will be
halted.

6. The engineer command, 43d Brigade, will join the advance of the 3d Battalion staff and at 0300 Sunday will blow up the bridge over the Bosut between Satnica and Casinci.

7. The Casinci operation must be completed by 1000 Sunday. Subsequently the country in the direction of Faucje and Slatinik will be vacated. Wounded and vehicles carrying booty will travel by way of Levanjska Varos.

8. I shall accompany the 1st Battalion as far as the edge of the forest west of Casinci. Report will be sent there when the objectives directed have been reached.

Death to the Usurpers!

Long live Tito, the liberator of Croatia from the foreigner!

Signature.

Remarks

1. The General order of the Reich Commander of the SS that no post be withdrawn without his express approval prevented the only possible solution, namely, the timely abandonment of Casinci.

2. Even energetic efforts to aid the platoon in Casinci would have been frustrated, as the enemy was too strong and his disposition extremely good. The platoon was sacrificed uselessly.

3. No punitive expedition into the Papuk mountains was undertaken; the requisite forces could not be assembled.

4. Casinci was the turning point of the partisan war. Thereafter, the partisans took the offensive and even attacked

more strongly garrisoned places which protruded inconveni-
ently into their territory and impeded their steady expansion.
Two months later fierce fighting took place for Nasice, which
changed hands repeatedly.

ATTACK ON LUDBREG
(See Sketches 5 and 2)

November 1943. The Bilo gora was occupied by partisans,
many of whom were also in the Ivancica mountains, where they
harassed the countryside bordering on Austria. Countermeasures
were taken by the 19th SS and Police Regiment in Maribor (Mar-
burg), Austria. To protect the communication line Varazdin -
Koprivnica, a company of German-Croatian police was stationed
in Ludbreg. Croatian army units and a special detachment of
the security service were in Varazdin, while Krizevci was occupied by a Croatian army company.

At 1600 hours, it was impossible to get any connection
whatever at Ludbreg on the state telephone system. The company commander sent a patrol with repairmen in the direction
of Koprivnica to discover the cause of the breakdown. They
returned one and a half hours later to report that they had
been fired upon. At the same time, the Croatian gendarme
post reported, "Partisans from the region of the Kalnik mountains are operating in the country around Ludbreg and have ordered the population to withdraw into their houses or leave
the locality. The gendarme post cannot maintain its position
and requests permission to join the company." Permission was
quickly granted, and the company was alerted and sealed off

the village. Partisans who had penetrated into it were
forced out. About midnight the situation became quiet, with
only slight combat activity on the periphery of the settlement.

The company was separated into groups, all of which set
out simultaneously and silently at 0200 to effect the break-
through in a surprise move. While security detachments advanced laterally along the Beduja river, the mass of the
company advanced in squad, moving in both directions along
the bank and the bed of the river until they were beyond the
encirclement ring of the partisans. The company commander
had designated Koprivnica and Kricevoi as rallying points,
and the Croatian gendarmes, who were familiar with the region,
were distributed among the various groups. The whole company
reassembled at the rallying points during the next few days
after suffering only about fifteen casualties. The action of
the company commander was approved by his superiors, since he
could not have held out till reinforcements arrived, owing to
lack of ammunition.

THE DESTRUCTION OF THE GARRISON OF CASMA
(See Sketches 6 and 2)

In May 1944 the garrison of Bjelovar consisted of one
Wehrmacht training battalion and about 500 men attending the
Croatian gendarme training center, which was located there.
Advance units, stationed in a line Gudovac - Narta - Veliki
Severin - Sandrovac - Veliki Troistvo, were in constant contact with partisan divisions from the Bilo gora. Those
companies of the gendarme school which had been advanced to
Grdjevo and Grubisno Polje in order to guard tree-felling
operations had to be recalled as they were in danger of being
cut off. Several partisan combat units were in the Moslavacka
mountains.

Altogether 700 men were stationed in Casma, composing
one battalion and a battery of the Croatian Army and a company of the German-Croatian police, while Dugo Selo was held
by a battalion staff and two companies of German-Croatian police. The Zagreb - Sisak - Novska - Brod and Zagreb - Ivanicgrad - Novska railroads were strongly guarded by the German and
Croatian forces. Both lines were utilized only during day-
light and under special precautions. There were minor attempts
at disturbance almost daily on both railway lines. The armed
escorts on the railway trains and with motor vehicle columns
were at least at company strength.

At noon on Tuesday, the garrison commander of Casma
reported by radio that strong partisan units had encircled
Casma and that he was expecting an attack at any hour. He
urgently requested assistance. The afternoon brought another
call for help. The attack had begun, and the partisans had
considerable numerical superiority and were well equipped.
Mortars were used by both sides. At the same time Bjelovar
reported a revival of enemy combat activity, the railway security headquarters at Sisak reported attacks on various
railway security detachments between Lekenik and Sisak, and
the railway security headquarters at Ivanicgrad reported
interruption of the railway stretch between Dugo Selo and
Ivanicgrad. Countermeasures were underway, but for the time
being train service was suspended.

To relieve Casma the only available battalion of German-
Croatian police, including a heavy machine gun and a trench
mortar platoon, was alerted and dispatched in trucks from
Zagreb during the night of Tuesday/Wednesday. It arrived in
Dugo Selo at 0600 and took along the battalion which was
stationed there. At the same time, the garrison commander of
Bjelovar was ordered to send support from his command to
Casma as quickly as possible. SS Gruppenfuehrer* Kammerhofer,
Himmler's representative, accompanied the battalion from

_____

* Equivalent to brigadier general.

Zagreb. Security detachments felt out the flanks enroute, and Klostar Ivanic was reached around noon. From there on sniper fire was received, and the advance came to a halt in the village of Mali Ivanic because of tenacious partisan resistance. The fighting intensified in the village, and the security detachments which had been sent out on both sides were attacked by strongly superior partisan forces and pressed back to the main unit, which was now also fired upon from the flanks. The Gruppenfuehrer now gave the order to break off the engagement and withdraw, which only a part of the column succeeded in doing before the approach of darkness, with heavy losses in officers, enlisted men and vehicles.

Casma was taken by the partisans during the same night. Not a man of its garrison escaped. The reinforcement detachment from Bjelovar, which was only of battalion strength, encountered strong resistance near Stefanje, against which it could make no headway. It therefore gave up the attempt to push forward to Casma. The Gruppenfuehrer's general staff officer computed the losses in and around Casma at thirty-five officers and more than 1,000 men. Casma remained in partisan hands.

FOUR SHORT STORIES
(See Sketches 1 and 2)

October 1943. To protect the Sarajevo area, one German-
Croatian police company was sent to Travnik, one to Mostar
and one to Rogatica. These spots had rail communications, and
the supply transports from Sarajevo were accompanied by small
escorts. The company commanders went to Sarajevo by rail every
two or three weeks to make their reports. In August 1943,
the company commander, a middle-aged district lieutenant of
the rural police, in accordance with orders given by the
district commander, negotiated with a representative of the
Chetniks from the nearby Zlatibor plateau. The Chetniks had
promised to aid in the fight against the Tito partisans in
the border region along the Drina river if certain ammunition
were delivered to them. Naturally they wanted the ammunition
first. The negotiations failed. Six weeks later, the lieutenant was taken from the train by partisans at the Praca railroad station. A search party sent from Rogatica found his
naked corpse on the same evening about two kilometers beyond
the railroad station. The tongue had been cut out and the
eyes put out. It could not be determined whether the culprits
where Chetniks or followers of Tito.

November 1943. The training battalion of the German

forces stationed in Sid, which lay thirty kilometers south
of Vinkovci, had received new recruits four weeks before.
An ideal training field, a practically level pasture with
a clear line of vision of about 1200 meters, was situated
about one and a half kilometers from Sid on the road Sid -
Sot - Ilok. The field was intersected by an almost dry
ditch, and on its northern edge was a small woods. The
1st Company reached the field at 0730, sent a security patrol into the little strip of woods as on other days, stacked
its weapons and prepared for early morning athletics. Sudden-
ly a burst of machine gun fire coming across the field from
a distance of about 800 meters poured into the men, who were
in formation , killing five and injuring eight of them and
throwing the rest into confusion. Everyone first sought
shelter. The firing ceased, and by the time the unit had
collected and recovered its weapons the two partisans who
had manned the light machine gun had reached the edge of the
woods, moving in a crouching position in the ditch, and had
disappeared in the direction of the Fruska gora.

February 1944. The German-Croatian police company sent
from Zagreb to Velika Gorica had reinforced the Croatian rural
police post in Buseveco with a machine gun section. The section scoured the outpost area, looking for partisans, who had
appeared here in isolated cases. Accompanied by his driver

and two escorts, the company commander drove to Busevceo
every second or third day. One day, while travelling at
high speed, they overtook three singing, slightly unsteady
Croats, who, although the horn was sounded, would not leave
the street and thus forced the driver to apply his brakes.
At this moment two shots were fired from some bushes quite
near to the street, instantly killing the district lieutenant.
The escorting men, who had been ready to fire, shot left and
right and the driver stepped on the gas. The three inebriates
had disappeared from the street. A few shots whistled behind
the vehicle without hitting it.

August 1944. The battle front had already reached Croatia
in a line from Osijek - Vukovar - Tuzla, and in the outpost
area of Zagreb south of the Save fire was occasionally opened
again in fights with partisans coming from the south and the
west. Partisans were also reported in the northerly mountain
slopes of the Zagrebacka gora, to the north of Zagreb. The
Security Service had set up a practice range for light machine
guns and submachine guns in a valley near Vrapce, five kilometers west of Zagreb. On the road that led to the range
were various small suburbs and a number of villas scattered
about the countryside. At 1315 a Security Service passenger
car, headed in the direction of the rifle range and occupied
by a driver, a commissioner and two technical sergeants, was

stopped at a turn in the road. The commissioner was shot twice and the other occupants, with revolvers pointed at them, put up thir hands. The two sergeants were taken to a nearby ville, but the driver, who had been ordered to bring the car to the front yard of the villa, maneuvered himself free in reverse gear and was able to speed away in the direction of Zagreb. In an on-the-spot investigation an immediately alerted detail of the Security Service established that the villa belonged to a respectable Zagreb business man, who had installed in it an old married couple as caretakers. That morning, several men from one of the small villages in the North had come to the couple, had chatted and asked for lunch and then had gone down to the road. Apart from the caretakers the villa was unoccupied at the time of the attack. It was burned to the ground and the old couple were removed to Zagreb. The two Security Service sergeants were never found. As soon as the car had escaped the partisans departed with them into the mountains.

DEFENSE AREAS
(See Sketches 1 and 2)

By the end of 1943, and in fact even before that, it
had become obvious that the growth of the partisan movement
in Croatia could not be stopped with the means available.
Extensive areas were completely under partisan control. In
the partisan territory in Bosnia, trains were running and
markets were held. Armament and equipment improved, as the
Allies were supplying the partisans by sea and by air. The
first bombs from Allied planes hit Zagreb in the spring, and
by the summer of 1944 the partisans themselves had a small
number of planes. The German theater of operations was
narrowing perceptibly.

The German Wehrmacht, supported by the Croatian Army,
directed all its efforts toward protecting the Cilly - Zagreb -
Belgrade and the Brod - Sarajevo and Vinkovci - Osijek rail
connections, which were so important for them. At the order
of the Reich Commander of the SS, the German-Croatian police
devoted themselves to the protection of the region inhabited
by ethnic Germans. The Croatian Army and the Croatian military police attempted to keep the area around the larger cities, above all around Zagreb, free of partisans. The bodyguard of the Poglavnik, a division of select men, and those

classes of trainees at the Bjelovar Gendarme School which
had graduated in May 1944 were committed for this purpose.
T he bodyguard regularly patrolled the Zagrebacka and Ivan-
cica mountain ranges and the Kalnik massif and kept open the
communication line Zagreb - Varazdin - Koprivnica - Bjelovar -
Zagreb. A German-Croatian police regiment protected the
Samobor region against action from the Gorjanci mountains.
There were further control groups in Sisak, Hrv. Kostainica,
Novska, Gradiska and Brod, while Banja Luka was heavily
garrisoned by units of the Croatian Army and of the German-
Croatian police. In Syrmia, the Osijek - Vinkovci - Ruma -
Petro - Varazdin region was held. The security zones in
Bosnia were around Tuzla and Sarajevo.

The German and Croatian combat units were on the defensive everywhere. Their food supplies were running low and
Croatian desertions increased. The Croatian population was
reserved and at times even hostile in its attitude. The
ethnic Germans began to fear for their lives and met the
situation by choosing the uncertain fate of evacuees in the
Reich.

Defensive Measures

Along the railway lines, especially at bridges, concrete
guard towers were constructed and manned by strong guard units

which kept the vicinity under observation, patrolled as far
as the next guard tower, repaired minor damages and mutually
supported one another. In the larger railroad stations,
emergency trains with technical personnel aboard were kept
ready to move.

On both sides of the tracks, the terrain was cleared of
all growth to a distance of 100 meters, and two empty lumber
flatcars were coupled before the locomotives of trains travelling on those stretches in order to explode possible mines
without danger to the train itself. Damaged cars were un-
coupled on the open way and tipped over the railway embank-
ment. At the end of the train was a car equipped with an anti-
aircraft gun to ward off low flying airplanes. Each train
was commanded by the senior officer present and each manned
car by the senior NCO. If the train was attacked by planes
or came under fire, all personnel took cover left and right,
prepared to open fire. Only after the railway patrol reported
that the line was safe, did the trains continue from station
to station. All passengers were instructed as to their conduct before the trip, and an inspector of the railway patrol
had command authority for all security measures.

BATTLES FOR NASICE
(See Sketches 2 and 7)

Partisan detachments from the Papuk gorje had occupied
the localities of Padgorac, Nasice and Fericanci in a surprise advance in June 1944 and had thus severed communications between Osijek and Virovitica. To relieve the three
towns, the following forces were committed from the Osijek
area:

The 3d German-Croatian Police Regiment, with one
company of engineers and a horse-drawn battery of four 77 mm
field guns.

The 1st Battalion of the 4th Police Regiment, which
was stationed in Djakovo.

One and one-half Croatian army battalions stationed
in Virovitica, which were reinforced with two officers and
sixty men from the gendarme training school in Bjelovar.

On Tuesday, the following march objectives had been
attained:

The main column, with the 1st and 2d Battalions of
the 3d Regiment, the company of engineers and two field guns
had reached the villages of Prandanovci and Koska. The
villages of Bizovac and Valpovo were free of partisans.

The first column on the left, consisting of the 3d

Battalion of the 3d Police Regiment and two guns, had reached
the village of Poganovci.

The detachment from Virovitica had reached the
village of Miklos and Cacinci.

The operational objectives for Wednesday were as follows:

The main column was to advance through Breznica
within combat range of Nasice.

The attack on Nasice was to be launched at dawn on
Thursday.

The first column on the left was to advance through
Budimci to Podgorac, which was to be taken on Thursday morning
at the latest.

Operating in the Bracevi region, the second column
on the left, consisting of the 1st Battalion of the 4th
Police Regiment from Djakovo, was to cover the attack of the
3d Battalion of the 3d Police Regiment on Podgorac.

The detachment from Virovitica was to occupy
Fericanci.

The operations progressed more or less according to
plan. Fericanci and Podgorac were taken on Wednesday evening
after initial resistance, but the resistance in Nasice on
Thursday was obstinate and abated only after the flank colums,
advancing from Podgorac and Fericanci, joined in the fighting
during the course of the afternoon. At about 1600, shook

colums of the 1st and 2d Battalions of the 3d Police Regiment,
covered by the supporting fire of heavy machine gun platoons
which had been brought up to within 400 yards, penetrated into
the town on both sides of the road Breznica-Nasice. The partisans fled into the nearby woods in the direction of Gradiste.
Nasice was searched, security detachments advanced into the
countryside toward the Papuk gorje and the outskirts of the
village were prepared for defense against night attacks.

For protection against counter-attacks, the following
forces remained in the area:

In Nasice, the 3d Police Regiment - minus its 3d
Battalion, the company of engineers, the battery, the platoon
from the Croatian Gendarme School at Bjelovar.

In the Orahovica - Feriosnoi - Zdemi region, one
Croatian army battalion from Virovitica.

In Podgorac, the 3d Battalion of the 3d Police Regiment.

In Djakovo, the 1st Battalion of the 4th Regiment.

All units were directed to protect the harvesting
activities of the population. The assignment was difficult
and heavy casualties were suffered as a result of the activities
of snipers. Surprise fire from small groups coming out of the
Papuk gorje kept the security detachments on the alert day and
night.

The events in Rumania made it necessary to defend the
Vukovar - Petro Varazdin - Zemun-Belgrade sector of the right
bank of the Danube. The 3d Police Regiment was committed for
this purpose and had to leave the Nasice district, its duties
being taken over by Croatian army units and the 1st Battalion
of the 4th Police Regiment. At the end of August, the partisans reconquered Nasice after a battle lasting three days.
The survivors of the overpowered garrison tried to break out
on the third night. Of the sixty personnel of the Croatian
gendarme detachment from Bjelovar, one officer and six men
returned.

EVEN BANJA LUKA PROVES IMPOSSIBLE TO HOLD
(See Sketch 2)

Banja Luka was intended as the seat of the Croatian
government, and construction work on two government buildings,
a bank and a large hotel had been completed. It was a town
of some 5,000-7,000 inhabitants, many of whom were Moslems.
On precipitous cliffs above the Vrbas River was an old
Turkish citadel with bastions and a clear field of fire
extending from 150 to 200 meters all around. The old section
of the city was of pure Turkish character and had numerous
bazaars and mosques. Sections of the narrow gauge railway
to Prijedor - Bos. Novi had ceased operating in August 1943,
and all traffic took place on the Okucani - Stara Gradiska -
Banja Luka road. To the right and left of this road, as far
as the Vrbas, were flourishing villages inhabited by ethnic
Germans, which were protected by a battalion of German-Croatian
police. Another company of German-Croatian police was in the
citadel and a battalion of Croatian mountain infantry in the
city. Wooded hills surrounded Banja Luka to the northwest,
west, south and east, and behind these hills lay solid partisan territory.

Banja Luka was a bottle neck. The city had to be held
to maintain Croatian prestige. Patrols in the vicinity and

as far away as Prijedor, where a Croatian army unit was
stationed, kept the countryside relatively safe. After
several small attacks on Banja Luka had been repulsed, combat activity around the town increased in May 1944, coupled
with incendiary actions in the ethnic German villages. A
major offensive was expected, and reinforcements were made
ready. Before they were ready to march, the partisans took
Banja Luka under artillery fire from positions in the hills
and launched a major attack. All approaches to Banja Luka
were blocked. Nevertheless, three days passed before the
partisans succeeded in occupying the town. The garrison
withdrew into the citadel and held out there for another
two days until reinforcements, composed of German and Croatian
army detachments supported by artillery, mortars and planes,
could free the town, relieve the garrison in the citadel and
force the partisans back into the mountains. In this fighting,
Brigadefuehrer von Summern, who was district commander of
Osijek, was killed as a result of a direct artillery hit on
his command post.

The reinforcement remained in Banja Luka for four weeks.
Then they were urgently needed elsewhere and withdrawn. The
attacks on Banja Luka recommenced immediately. Under the
pressure of these attacks, Banja Luka was finally evacuated

and the troops of its garrison employed in protecting the
Sisak - Dubica - Nova Gradiska railway line. The ethnic
German population of the villages along the Banja Luka - Bos.
Gradiska road were evacuated to Germany and Austria.

October 1944 (See Sketch 1)

The Balkan front was collapsing. Rumania had been lost
in August 1944. Greece had to be abandoned and the German
troops which had been committed there fought their way
laboriously through the high mountain chain between the
Serbian and Albanian-Montenegrin areas to the bridges over
the Drina River. The way through Belgrade was barred, but
to the east of Sarajevo an SS corps held the Drina crossing
open. The German Army of Greece heavily dragged its way
through Croatia to an assembly area in Austria, and behind
it the battlefront advanced to a line Budapest - Vukovar -
Drina River. Dubrovnik (Ragussa) and Mostar were evacuated.
Partisan units took over sectors of the frontlines in Croatia,
and one Russian corps sufficed to support the slowly advancing
front.

About 100,000 men were under arms on the German side in
Croatia, more than two-thirds of them employed in protecting
the communication lines and areas behind the battlefront against
the partisans. Although at first only one-fifth of the autonomous State of Croatia was in the hands of the Allies, hardly

one-tenth of what remained was under relatively secure control by the Germans, thanks to partisan activity. This one-tenth of Croatia tied down the remnants of the army that had retired from Serbia under Generaloberst von Weichs* who, with his staff, had constructed air raid shelters in the Croatian Ministry of Health building in Zagreb.

The main enemy drive was directed from Budapest to Vienna. Croatia was no longer of interest to the Allies, as the German forces tied up there were an encircled army, whose surrender could be awaited without necessitating any special sacrifices. These German forces were also subject to Hitler's order not to yield a foot of ground, but sooner or later they would be completely cut off and would collapse.

Tito was the victor in Croatia. As his reward he requested and received authorization to organize Yugoslavia under his own rule. He had learned his lesson from what had happened to Rumania. Tito is a communist, but he is also a Croatian Yugoslav. His counterpart, Ante Pavelic, firmly maintains his Croatian nationalism in Argentina and carefully fosters his relations with those Ustashas who have emigrated to the West.

---

* Equivalent to full general.

CONCLUSIONS

No decisive success resulted from the anti-partisan action in Croatia. It did not lead to the suppression of the partisan movement, and yet this very suppression should have been the major objective in Croatia were to be enabled to develop healthily.

Since this objective, the eradication of the partisan movement was not achieved in spite of the fact that in 1943 a large proportion of the population was quite ready to support a promising campaign against the partisans, anti-partisan operations had to be limited to warding off interference with the supply lines to the front and the communications zone. The Germans tried to carry out this task both by offensive and defensive measures, but the course of the war on the eastern front forced them in 1944 to restrict themselves to defensive action and brought about the gradual collapse of all anti-partisan warfare.

Despite this logical course of events, the following lessons can be drawn from this chapter of the war:

1. Compromises result in half measures. The German regular police, who were commissioned to activate a German-Croatian police force, were taken by surprise when given this task. Experience had admittedly been gained in Poland, in

Russia and also in the rest of Yugoslavia, but conditions
in Croatia had a different aspect.

The police organizations in the occupied eastern territories were executive agencies of the German administrative
bodies which had been set up there. Their focal point was
the cities, where the majority of the German police really
were needed. To combat the partisans, specific SS- and Police
regiments were activated and committed.

Croatia, on the other hand, was an allied land. It
willingly changed from Italian to German supervision, since
it felt that it would receive more effective aid from the
Germans in establishing its own government than it had received from the Italians. When German supervision began,
the autonomous State of Croatia already had its own Croatian
administration and, in the rural police and city police, its
own executive agencies, to support which Ustasha forces stood
ready.

For the German-Croatian police organization, which had
to be newly activated, the right thing therefore would have
been to assume those missions which Croatian agencies were
not capable of handling, namely, anti-partisan activities.
The organization should have been shaped specifically for
this purpose. Instead, the organization of the German police
in Croatia was a compromise based on the normal purpose of a

police force, the protection, on the one hand, of the peaceful segment of the population and, on the other, the wartime
necessity of offensive action against partisans in Croatia
and their eradication if possible. In the activation stage,
the idea of the protective function led to the scattering of
the police force in small units and at places where Croatian
rural police had already been committed for the same purpose,
thereby restricting them to defensive missions.

2. Well directed partisan movements are like a cancerous
growth. Once they are recognized as such, radical countermeasures must be taken. If the fight is limited to the mere
amputation of a few odd tentacles, the growth will continue
to spread rapidly and sooner or later will destroy the attacked organism.

It was only gradually recognized that Tito's partisans
had a unified leadership, under which they worked toward a
positive goal. The central authorities in Berlin very un-
willingly and hesitantly accepted this fact. It did not fit
into the overall picture desired by top circles. Under the
influence of the decisive defeats on the eastern front, Berlin
first took the viewpoint that the situation in Croatia was
being exaggerated. Nonetheless, in order to do something,
the National Department of Security sent SS Obergruppenfuehrer

von der Bach-Zalewski*, the newly-appointed Inspector General
for Partisan Operation, to Croatia. He spent two days re-
ceiving voluminous reports and then gave it as his opinion
that, compared with the eastern front, fighting the partisans
in Croatia was child's play, pointing out that the partisans
never made a stand but ran away whenever they were energetically attacked. It was the only visit that von der Bach-
Zalewski paid Croatia, but the consequences of his report
were that the central authorities in Berlin only most re-
luctantly and hesitatingly recognized the unsuitability of
the initial organization. When the formation of mobile police
regiments was finally approved, much valuable time had been
lost.

3. In 1943 the participation of the Wehrmacht in combatting the partisans consisted of relief operations, which
aimed at and achieved a temporary alleviation of the over-all
situation but were unsatisfactory in their ultimate result
because steps to establish the lasting security of the region
gained in combat did not follow, so that the partisans were
able to reoccupy these territories in a very short space of
time and exercise increased pressure on the population.

The objective of every operation against a region that is
already under partisan control must be to secure this region

* Lieutenant general of the SS.

permanently against partisan activity. A well-considered,
limited objective is a categoric prerequisite for success.
To aim at too much with weak forces leads to the dissipation
of the forces, useless sacrifices and failure.

The mission is not completely fulfilled when a partisan
district has been combed and resistance broken; it is at
this point that the more difficult part of the job commences.
The partisans must be prevented from reassembling in their
old hideouts and resuming their earlier activity. The best
means to force the partisans out of their old resorts is to
occupy the resorts and thus undermine their previous position
from the inside. If this succeeds, they soon lose organized
control and striking power. The majority of the partisans
were men who had been recruited compulsorily from the immediate
vicinity. If the partisans permanently lost a focal region,
many of these members reverted to peaceful village life.
Small detachments and individuals could have been hunted
down by special units, and the population would have participated in this hunt, just as they supported the advances
into partisan territory as long as they could hope that the
Germans would remain in the raided area.

4. Just as is the case with air defense and chemical
warfare, anti-partisan action is a specific field within the
overall conduct of war. It requires co-operation between the

armed forces, the police and the national administration
in the country affected. The sooner systematic work begins,
the greater will be the chances of success. The necessary
collaboration must be securely organized before partisan
battalions are formed.

Since partisans appear only in occupied territories, it
is advisable to organize a planning staff for the respective
territory before it is occupied. The preparatory duties of
this body would be to collect reports, to investigate local
conditions and to make available the necessary tactical units.
Upon occupation of the territory, this staff must take all
measures to combat partisans and to execute these measures
until the final objective inhabiting the territory. The German general accredited to the government in Zagreb was not given
enough authority, and the Armeegruppe* in Belgrade had more
pressing problems.

5. The peculiar nature of partisan warfare requires the
following organizational arrangements:

a. A quickly and reliably functioning communication
net to collect and evaluate reports from the troops committed
to action, from the administration that had been set up and
from the threatened population, and to supplement these reports by information gathered through its own channels.

_____
* A reinforced corps.

b. Special troops /Jagdtruppen/ which can be
thrown into the threatened area at the first sign of partisan
activity. These troops do not require a long period of military training but are most effective if they equal or if
possible excel the partisans in mobility, self-sufficiency,
camouflaging ability and instinct. Members of the indigenous
population are useful, since they have basic similarities
with the partisans in many respects and are familiar with the
locality. The weapons and equipment of these troops should be
as light as possible.

c. A well trained and well equipped motorized combat force, to break resistance. This force must be so organized that it can be used effectively even in very small units.
Often only a machine gun nest will block a road or prevent
the removal of a road obstacle, and a small detachment with
one or two guns and a section of engineers, accompanying the
advance guard of a column, will suffice for the speedy removal
of such blocks. Pack animals are useful for operations in
mountainous territory. Instead of pack animals, the partisans used prisoners of war and the civilian population, including women and children.

6. If the German-Croatian police were to have fulfilled
the mission listed under 5,b, above, the gendarme and police

b. Special troops /Jagdtruppen7 which can be
thrown into the threatened area at the first sign of partisan
activity. These troops do not require a long period of military training but are most effective if they equal or if
possible excel the partisans in mobility, self-sufficiency,
camouflaging ability and instinct. Members of the indigenous
population are useful, since they have basic similarities
with the partisans in many respects and are familiar with the
locality. The weapons and equipment of these troops should be
as light as possible.

c. A well trained and well equipped motorized combat force, to break resistance. This force must be so organized that it can be used effectively even in very small units.
Often only a machine gun nest will block a road or prevent
the removal of a road obstacle, and a small detachment with
one or two guns and a section of engineers, accompanying the
advance guard of a culumn, will suffice for the speedy removal
of such blocks. Pack animals are useful for operations in
mountainous territory. Instead of pack animals, the partisans used prisoners of war and the civilian population, including women and children.

6. If the German-Croatian police were to have fulfilled
the mission listed under 5,b, above, the gendarme and police

officers and sergeants arriving from Germany in batches, as
well as the newly-recruited Croatian personnel, should not
have been distributed among police companies which were per-
forming sentry duty or among even smaller units, but rather
should have been held together in a police training battalion.
The compact battalion unit is the best guarantee that the
training objective will be attained. The battalion commander
can completely devote himself to this task in daily co-operation with the companies. The battalion type unit also makes
possible a much better utilization of time, since the security
and labor services scarcely require more personnel for a
whole battalion than for a single company.

7. Once training battalions have been assembled at the
headquarters centers, they must be transferred to newly
cleared partisan territory, the green troops from the very
outset must adjust themselves completely to the peculiarities
partisan warfare, even if there is no immediate danger.
The sooner green troops absorb the instinctive awareness of
danger that is a feature of partisan proximity, the sooner
will they be serviceable for offensive partisan combat.

8. The characteristics essential in troops whose job
is to combat and eradicate partisans are frugality, readiness
for action at short notice, resourcefulness in forest and
mountain areas and readiness to engage in man-to-man combat.

The best training area is the danger zone; the best training medium is danger.

Training must begin with safeguarding of billets, supervision of the immediate vicinity, setting of traps and am-
bushes, exercises in feinting movements and large-scale
patrols to track down partisan hide-outs. The first thing to
be practiced is proficiency in what will be essential in this
type of work. Formal training, to which the German NCO is
partial as reminiscent of his own peacetime training, should
take a position of secondary importance. (Gaps in the training will be gradually eliminated. In this type of training,
individual casualties during the instruction period must be
accepted as an unavoidable hazard. Lack of supply trains
and primitive quarters in temporary billets of bivouacks
should be the normal form of life for these troops. Officers
and NCO's who can not adapt themselves to such a guerilla-
like existence must be culled out ruthlessly.

Excellent rations must compensate for other privations,
and recreation and relaxation under urban conditions must be
provided at regular intervals. Through remaining in the
danger zone, a green unit of this type will develop initially
into what might be called a forest ranger corps /Waldaufklae-
rungskorps/. Its transformation into a disciplined service
unit, so far as outward appearance is concerned, must be
reversed for the recreational sojourns in the city.

It should not be felt that such a life is too much
to be expected of green troops. It would have succeeded
in Croatia. The majority of the Croatian personnel was
already familiar with such a life in one form or another.
It was new only to the majority of the German leaders. However, what the partisans managed the troops committed to combat them should also have been able to accomplish. There
were officers among the rural police who were fitted for
such activity. Selection should not have been based on
seniority. In addition, there should have been a versatile
training inspector, thoroughly conversant with existing conditions, who would not merely have inspected but rather would
have shared the life of such a battalion for three or four
days at a time, and issued no written orders but rather ad-
vised the battalion commander. There would have been certain
difficulties to surmount, especially in respect to supply
and administration, but they would have been no greater than
in a front sector. Placed in a position where they are com-
pelled to fend for themselves, green troops will learn in
four weeks things that they never learn in city garrisons, or
learn only when their post is surrounded and they are anni-
hilated in their first battle.

THE BILO GORA OPERATION AS A TEST CASE
(See Sketch 2)

After troops in the strength of a Wehrmacht division
had been mobilized for the penetration assault on the Bilo
gora and the Papuk, the operation should have been executed
not as a relief but rather as a mopping up action. Besides
the military measures, the preparations for the operation
should have included plans to insure that once partisan resistance had been overcome the territory covered would not
again fall into partisan hands. Effective combat units
should have been left in the operations zone until it was
sufficiently secured against immediate reoccupation by the
partisans.

The previous protective system for the outlying villages
around the operations zone should have been abandoned temporarily, and all available companies of the German-Croatian
police should have been consolidated in battalions, which
should have been transferred to the partisan quarters in the
Bilo gora and the Papuk. Adequate numbers of troops could
have been spared for such an occupation. The German-Croatian
police even at the beginning of the operation numbered some
10,000 men. If we assume that a training regiment would have
contained three battalions, each battalion having four com-

panies of 120 - 130 riflemen, every man armed with either
a rifle or a submachine gun, two regiments would have required fewer than 3500 officers and men. Since recruiting
in Croatia progressed quickly, this commitment would have
been offset by replacements in two months at the most.

One regiment could have been activated from the district
of Zagreb and could have established itself in the villages
of Zrinsky, Pisanica veliki and Pisanica mali. The other regiment would have had to be assembled from the garrisons of
the Osijek district and billeted in the Papuk mountains, the
terrain on the Papuk plateau being ideally suited for a troop
drill ground and artillery range. To activate the two regiments would have called for a masterpiece of improvisation.
This necessity would not have arisen if, from the outset,
new recruits had been retained in training battalions instead
of being distributed among the detached companies, where their
effectiveness was blunted in training and labor services.

A commander should have been appointed to control all
units which remained in the combed area to dislodge the partisans, and his mission would have been, with a large degree
of independence, to take all suitable measures to prevent
reoccupation of the area by the partisans. Any locality and
region in which the formation of a new partisan nucleus was
reported should have been occupied immediately by a sufficiently

strong troop unit and an interrogation group of the SS security service, which could then have been withdrawn in a
relatively short while. During this time, food and so forth
could have been requisitioned locally.

Further Plans

With the Bilo gora and Papuk secured, the clearance of
the Moslavacka gora and the Psunje would no longer have been
very difficult. New police training battalions would have
had to be sent up to this area. The Fruska gora was likewise
a minor objective. If the unification of the partisan forces
had been prevented permanently in these areas, the entire
region between the Drava and the Save to a great extent would
have been secure against partisan influence. Available forces
would have had to mop up the Save lowlands and establish
themselves as a barrier before the Bosnian mountains. The
clearing of these mountains required separate plans based on
new premises.

The Croatian Population

The treatment of the native population required careful
consideration. The inhabitants of the villages along the
borders of partisan territory received little protection from
the German-Croatian police units. If they temporarily
succumbed to partisan influence, this was a consequence of

their defenselessness. The population within the partisan territory succumbed to absolute coercion. To regard them collectively as criminal partners of the partisans was neither just nor wise.

/s/ Karl Gaisser

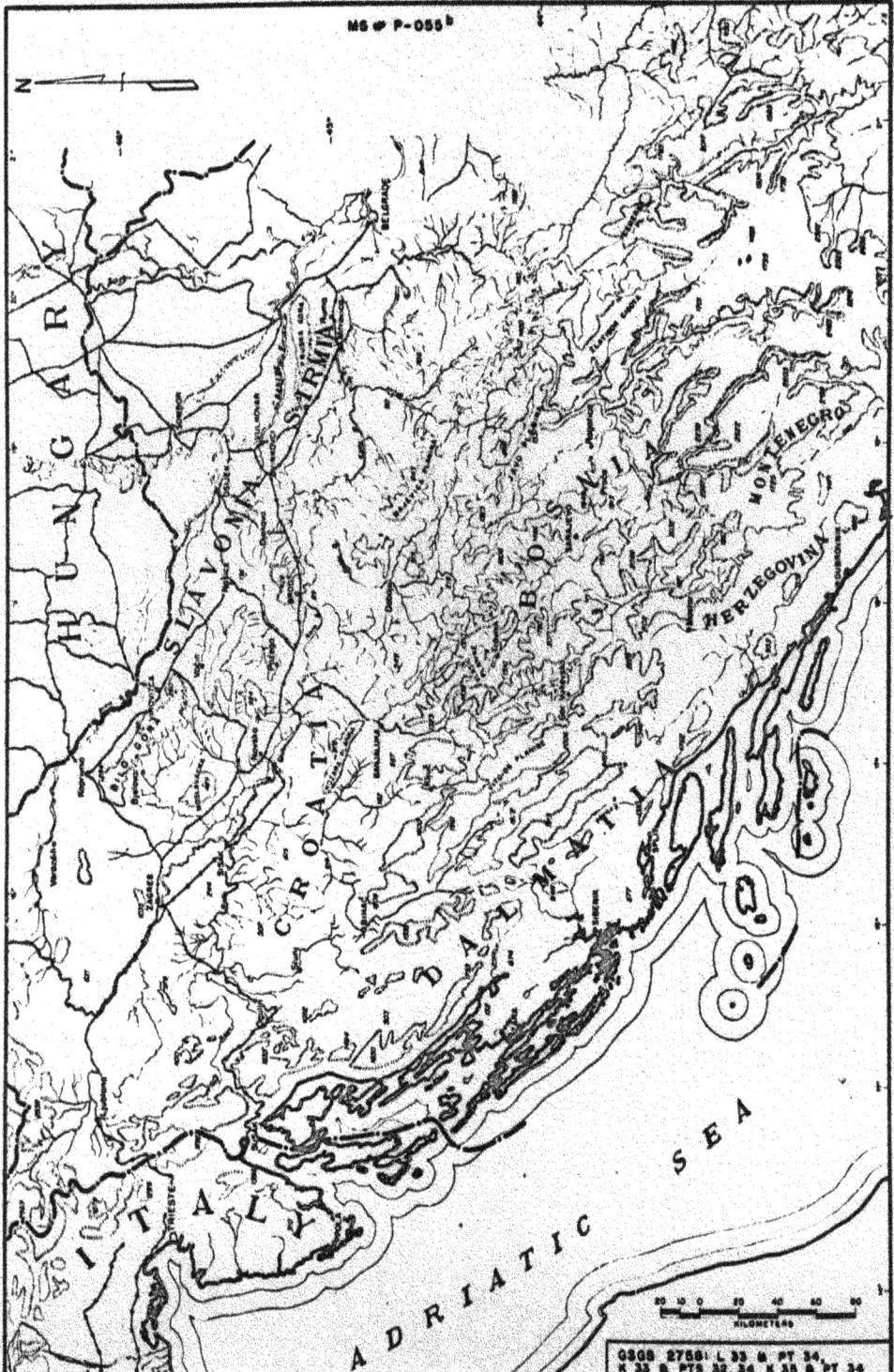

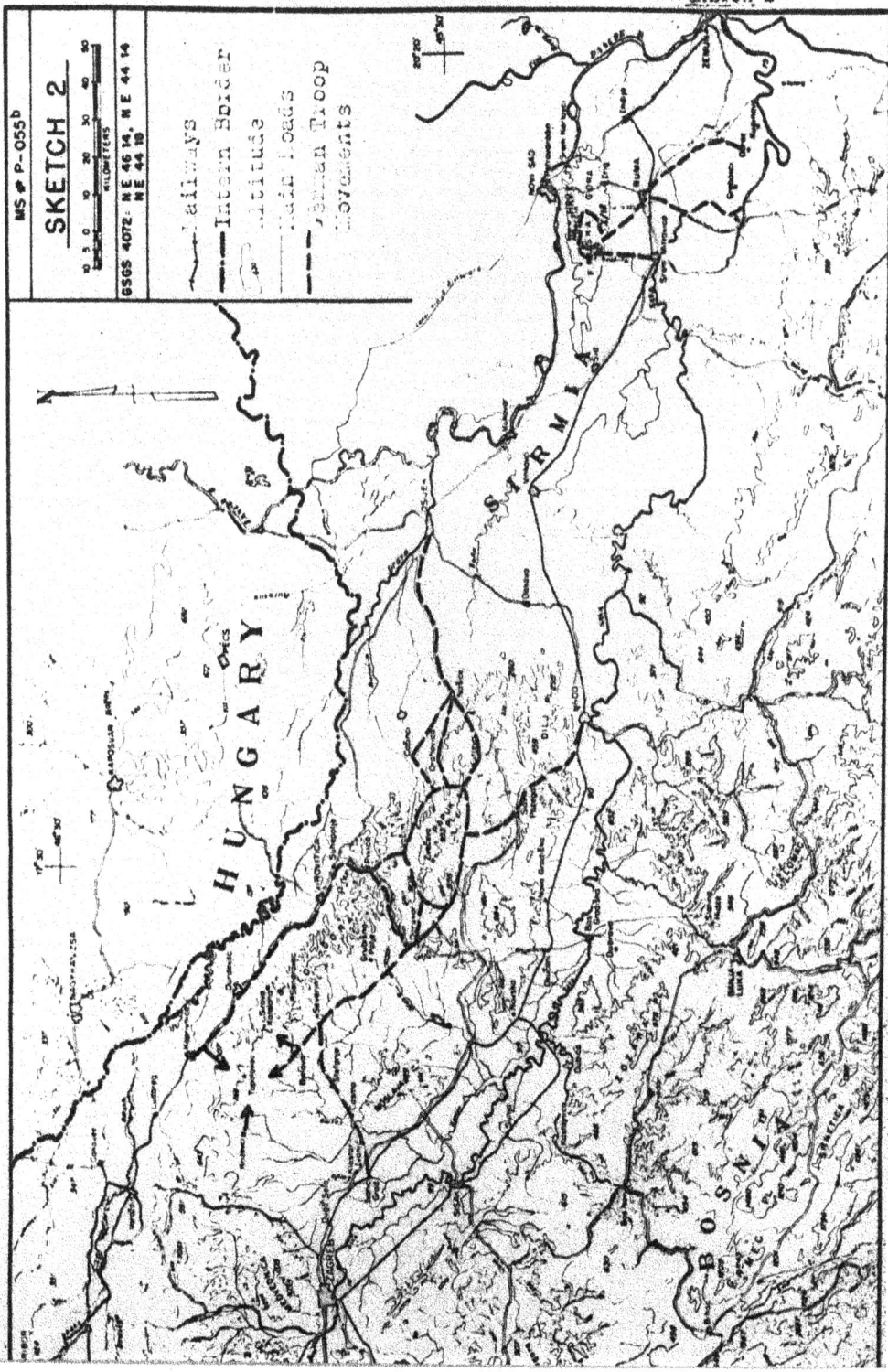

SKETCH 2

SKETCH 2

GSGS 4072: NE 46 14, NE 44 14
NE 44 10

—— Railways
━━━ Intern Border
⌒ Altitude
—— Main Roads
- - - German Troop
       Movements

KILOMETERS

HUNGARY

S I R M I A

B O S N I A

GSGS: 4396: 32

.... Marching routes & positions
of the partisans

Surprise attack on the Signal Communication Platoon of the
area in particular con- 54th Rifle...

Probable route of march
of march of the partisans who made
the surprise attack

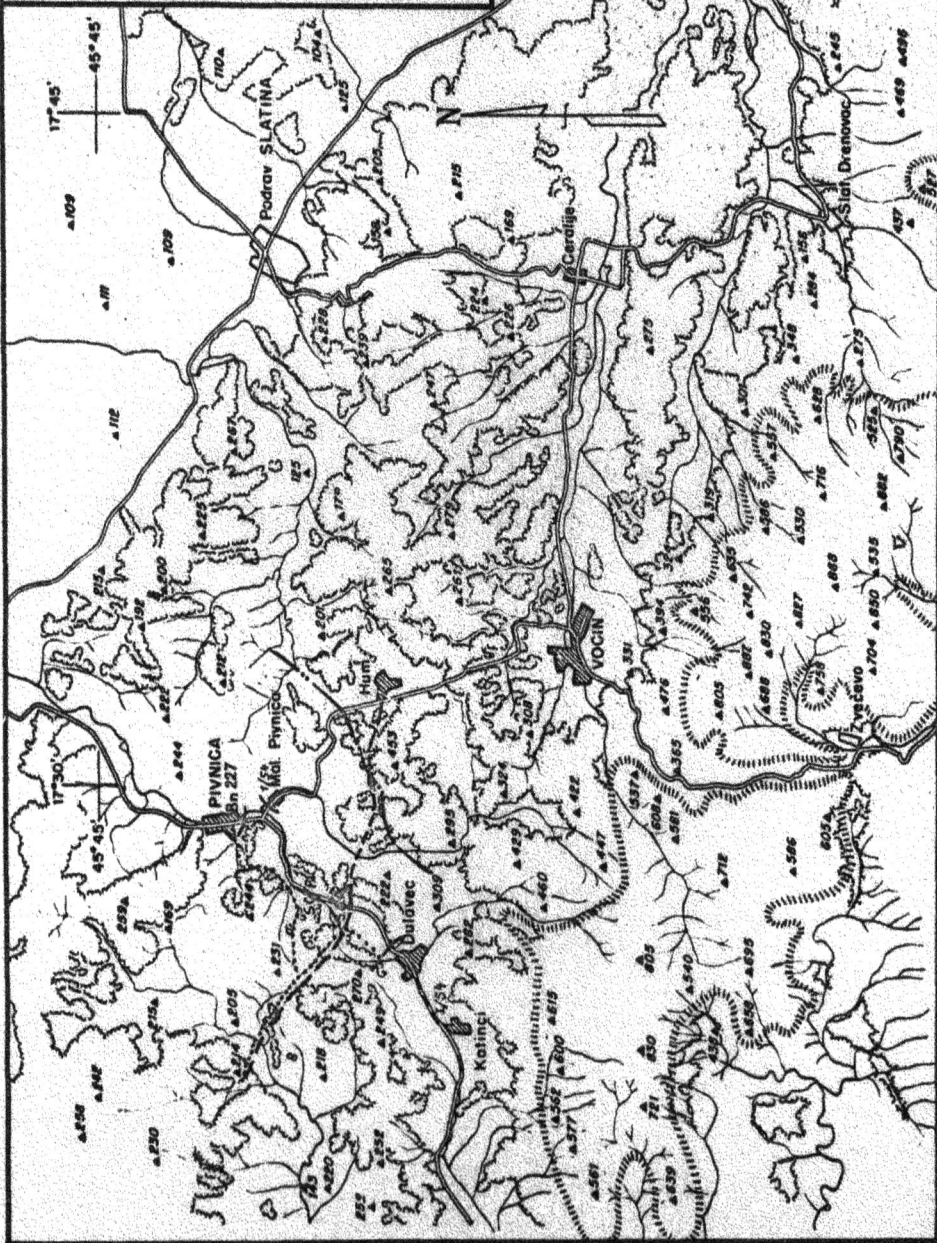

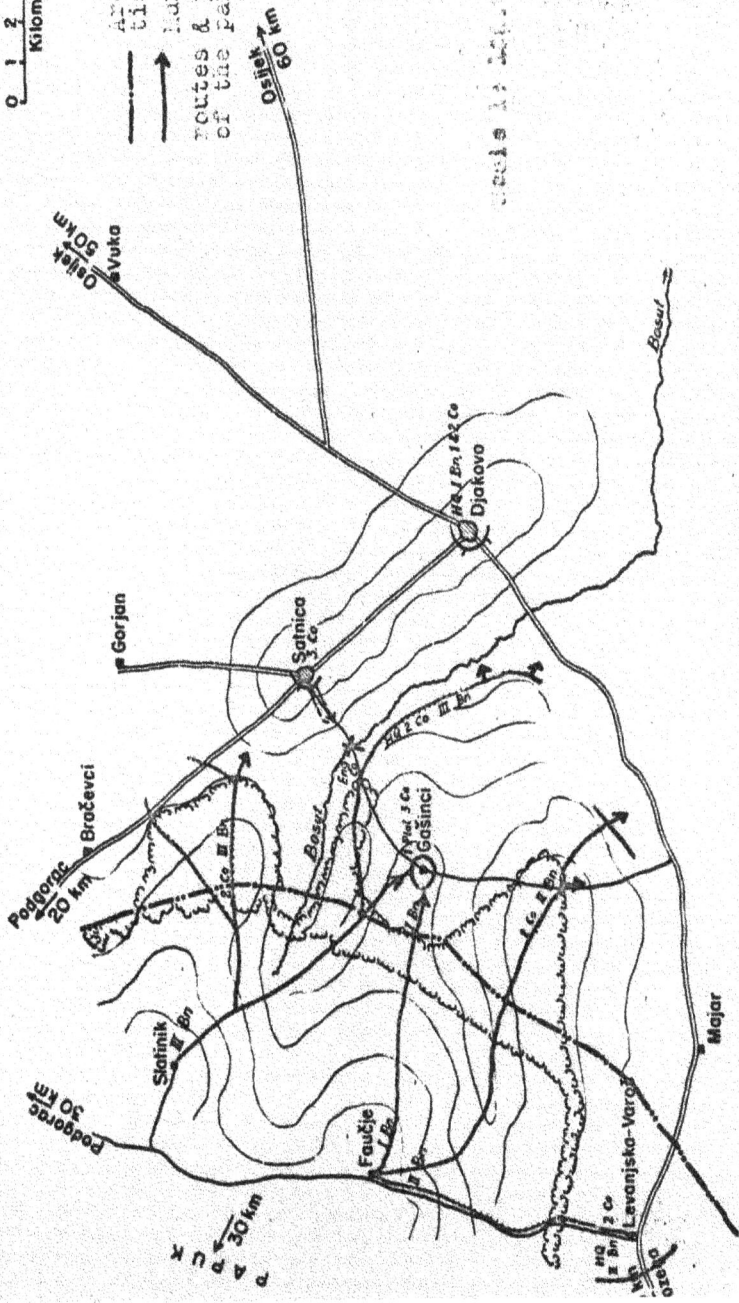

SKETCH 4

0 1 2 3 4 5
Kilometers

Area in partisan control

Marching

routes & positions
of the partisans

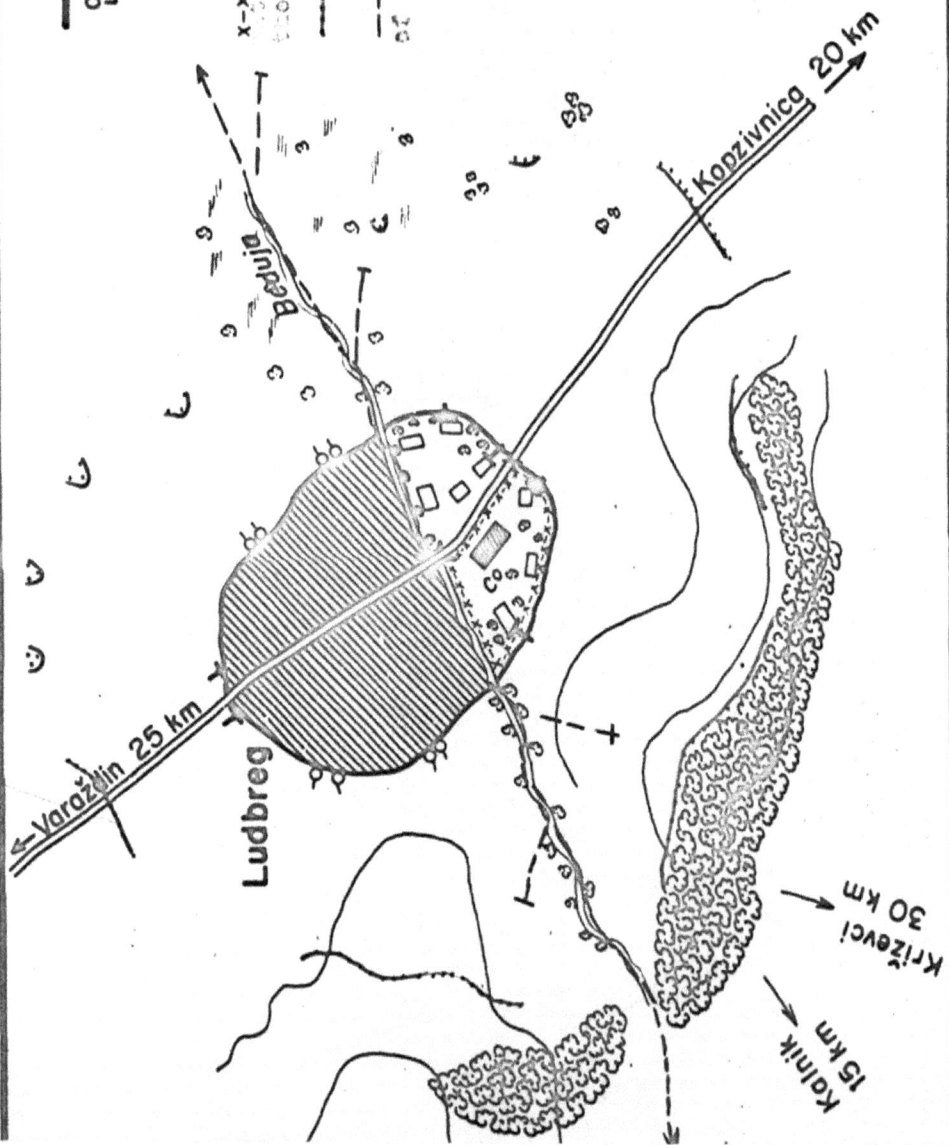

SKETCH 5

METERS

0   50   100   150   200   250

x-x-x-x Area protected
         by the security
         company

Ludbreg

Bednja

←Varaždin 25 km

Koprivnica 20 km

Križevci 30 km

Kalnik 15 km

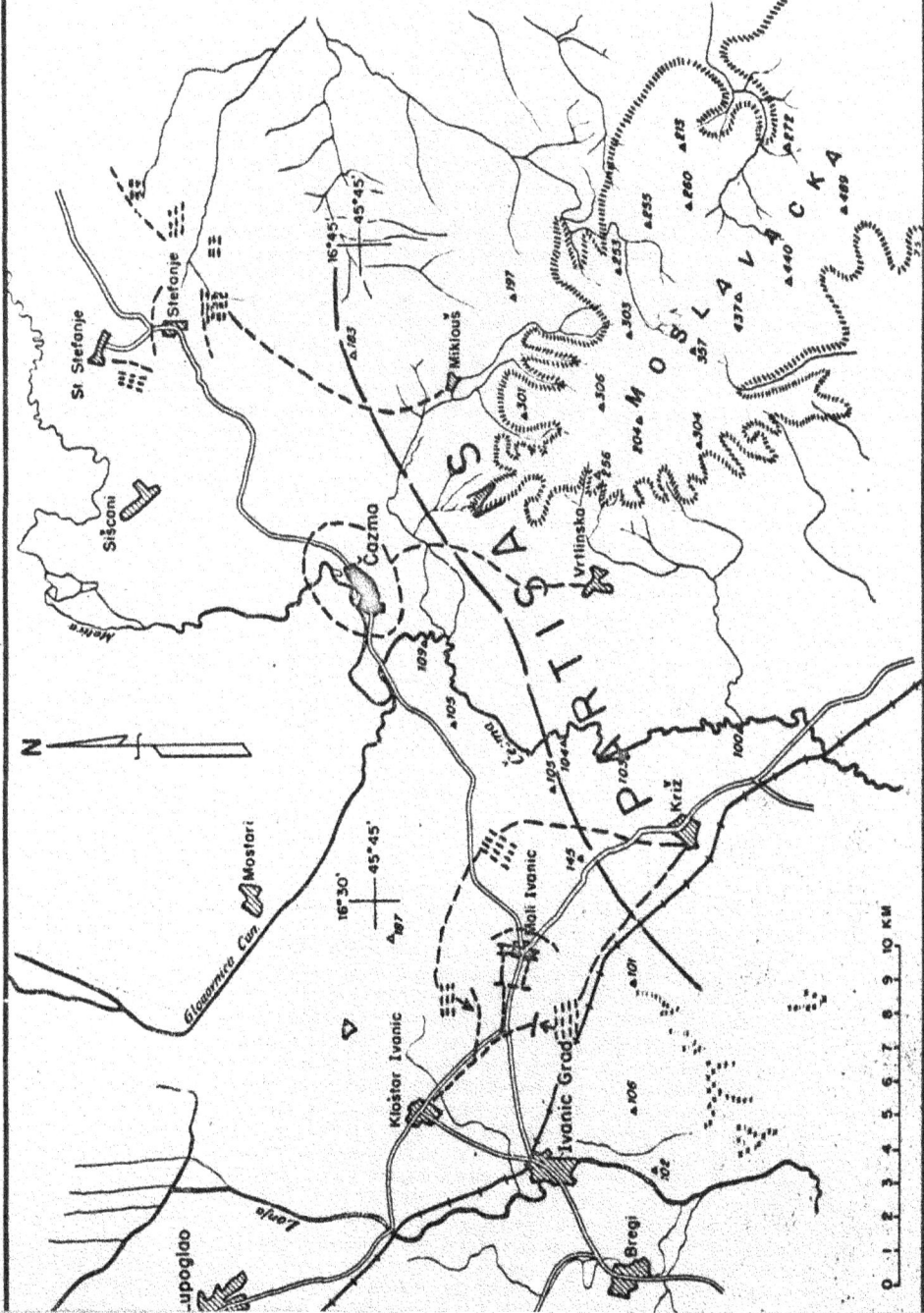

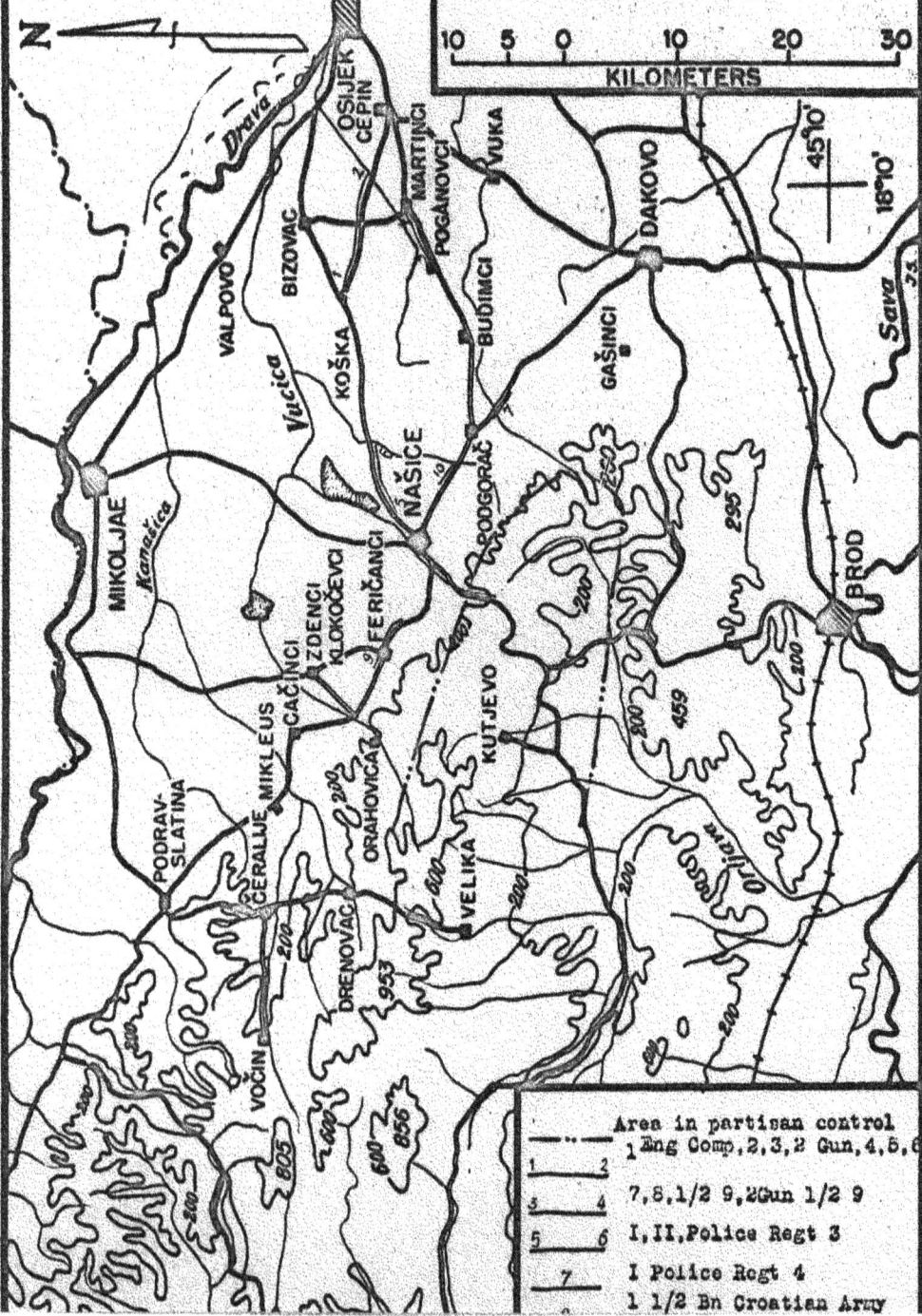

MS # P-055

SKETCH 7

KILOMETERS
10   5   0   10   20   30

Area in partisan control
1 Eng Comp,2,3,2 Gun,4,5,6
7,8,1/2 9,2Gun 1/2 9
I,II,Police Regt 3
I Police Regt 4
1 1/2 Bn Croatian Army

www.ingramcontent.com/pod-product-compliance
Lightning Source LLC
Chambersburg PA
CBHW050355100426
42739CB00015BB/3408